73

Our Poison Horse

ଓ

by Derrick C. Brown

Write Bloody Publishing
America's Independent Press

Austin, TX

WRITEBLOODY.COM

Our Poison Horse

© 2014 Write Bloody Publishing

No part of this book may be used or performed without written consent from the author, except for critical articles or reviews.

Write Bloody
First Edition
ISBN: 9781938912535

Cover art by Jennifer Heuer
Proofread by Melinda Aguilar
Edited by Heather Knox, Mindy Nettifee, Gary Lovely, Jene Guiterrez, Cristin O'keefe Aptowicz and Anis Mojgani
Interior layout by Ashley Siebels
Cover & Author photo by Jessica Blakeley

.

Type set in Bergamo from www.theleagueofmoveabletype.com

Printed in Tennessee, USA

Write Bloody Publishing
Austin, TX
Support Independent Presses
writebloody.com

To contact the author, send an email to writebloody@gmail.com

MADE IN THE USA

For Eugene Mirman

OUR POISON HORSE

OUR POISON HORSE

TO HOLLER AMONG THE LIVING

TEXAS ON A SATURDAY NIGHT

THE POET VS. TOO MANY DRINK TICKETS

DARKNESS, EARLY TO THE PARTY

WHY MATT TAKES OFF HIS SHIRT IN
EVERY ART GALLERY

ROMANCE IS AN UNSUPERVISED GO-KART TRACK

ATX-73
DEPARTMENT OF O.P.H.

TO HOLLER

AMONG THE LIVING

WRITE BLOODY TACTICAL MANUALS
EST. 2004

THE STARGAZER IS DYING

And I'm telling you to live, to hang on.
I'll change the low water in your vase.
We can jam you back into the ground.

Spring is in approach.
The squirrels are being photographed.
There is a flood of sunlight coming,
the rivers are rising for swimming.

Why do you give such sweet smells
before going?
This color is all you get to do?

You made the dead house wonder.
You made this gaze bloom.
We carried your beauty to others
and said,

Can you imagine seeing this in the wild?
Can you imagine how beautiful
it would be if it were still alive?

GRACKLES IN WAR LIGHT

I have never seen the light swallow
the field like it did last night.
I couldn't leave the barn.

Have you ever seen lightning dance that fast,
so pissed and ready for death,
the night goes all hard-on, strobing along,
wanting to take some farmer down?

I wished I could go into the clouds
and watch from above: the descent
of all the bright war light,
imploding gods,
angelic powder kegs alight,
howitzers hammering down
over this little
yellow
house.

Soon, the storm holds and the Grackles
perch on the barbed wire.

The wind winds down
in surrender.

A battered black chair has landed in the field.
I can't help but think it is for me.

If I sit upon it,
will the winds rise?

The great oak
leans alone on the hill, staring down
the field, full of bloodthirsty birds.
How can there be so many vultures
and still so many rabbits?

One vulture lifts from the tree,
wings as wide as Christ,
and holds fast in the headwind, still
and high, frozen in the air,
head down,
feathers rifling. Dressed up
for the occult hazing, he goes nowhere.
Just holds.
Not hunting. Floating post-storm.

Is this a break from the constant job
of waiting,
waiting for food,
for blood and murder,
for carcass and pickings?

I swear he is having fun.

Yes, the other vultures never understood him,
watching their special brother with disdain
as he does nothing in the low gale.

How they wish he would stick to his role
and wait for the lightning to take down a beast
so they could fill their bellies and live a life
of waiting for something awful
to feel full.

THE RUINED LIFE

Your life is ruined
when one lost person becomes a loved, low song
and you stop searching
for new music, convinced it will all sound the same.

Your life is ruined
when you won't make her dinner
because you hate dirty dishes
more than you love her.

Your life is ruined
when you hoped the violence
you saw in him
would protect you from the world, and how sad that it did.

Your life is ruined
when someone makes you choose
science or miracles
without seeing how well they party.

Your life is ruined
when you realize too late that the magic it takes
to change someone
exhausts all your magic.

Your life is ruined
when all your friends tell you to get married
because it makes buying a house easier,
but you never see them 'cause it demands so much work.

Your life is ruined
when you begin to rebuild your home
before the last bomb falls and the war
is declared over.

Your life is ruined
when people holding hands
while riding bikes
just seems dangerous.

300 BONES

Roy Sullivan still holds the record
for being struck by lightning 7 times over the span of 20 years
and surviving. He left this earth by his own hand.
The lightning could not take him down.

I can imagine the first time it found him.
Out in his pickup truck at night,
remembering that a truck can diffuse lightning
but not if the window is down—Vajam!
feeling the first blast of light wash over him fast
like a fire hose gushing electricity, turning him all x-ray,
hands steaming, hair sizzling, heart shock-jacked, hot organs huddled up,
a left hook from the heavens.

The second and third time it struck him
it all felt sudden and ridiculous.
An impossible stroke of luck.
The news trucks showing up.
Mr. Lightning Rod. The Human Conductor. Roy, the Lightning Sucker.
Priests in their hickey hiding collars, using his tale as allegory,
telling kids that God physically punishes the wicked
when we step out of his love.
 The fourth and fifth time, people distanced themselves from Roy.
Scared of what ire he draws from the angels
and all the forces of the heavens.
He was gunpowder.
He was a marked target.
His boots flying from his feet.
Laces still tied.

A jug of water to douse his burning hair,
always at the ready in the passenger side.
His wife leaving him after he was struck.
The news turning his magic, common.

The sixth time. No one came.

Roy's fingernails black and gray. A scar down his shin. Hair crisped.
The doctors gave him aloe vera and told him to be careful.
They couldn't explain why he wasn't dead.
Roy moved through the town like a ghost
even when the sun was shining.
No return to normalcy when the world christens you as bad luck.

The seventh time.
Roy noticing thunder clouds rolling towards him,
daring them to speak. "Try and take me. Try and take me away."

A smile welling up in his burnt molars when he feels it start to sprinkle.
It strikes. It bullets down, whips his legs out. He is unconscious.
His suspender buckles, like stoves.
He pulls himself through the mud
to the passenger side of his truck,
dumps the water on his head.

One reporter returned to the emergency room
for a follow up story on Roy's impossible world record:
"7 times, Roy. Aren't you scared that you've pushed your luck?
Most people die from one.
Will you still go outside to work if there's a storm?"

Roy replied in simple southern notes:
"I will still try to."

I can imagine the reporters asking Roy, "What was it like?"

Roy sitting up and clearing his throat.
"What was it like? It hurt. It all hurt.
The lightning and everything else.
But I'm glad it happened.
I feel strong. I feel strong the way you feel strong from love,
and I see now that I can't go
until I get it all out. I am so full.
I have to get it all out. If God wants it back, he picked the wrong fight.
It's mine.

It has always been mine.
My heart beats on.
My bones are strong.
Five times stronger than steel,
not poetically—scientifically.

We are born with 300 bones, and we die with 206.
This means
there are bone guzzlers in the shadows.
All dressed up in *No, thank you's* and *Get lost's.*
They will come for you,
and you must douse them in jars of blood, cum, flowers, yes, color,
fast power, truth stripped, hard loss, tongue kissing, sorrows bazaar,
flight, love, love, love, and 100,000 beats.

Money broke up with me a long time ago.
Do I still live like a low budget shower scene Psycho scream?
I still try to.

I stopped reading the bible
and started believing in miracles—
alive is a miracle.
Your life is medicine to someone.
You gotta go find the sick.
 Do I still dance even when all the great dance halls are all closing down?

One dance floor closes down
and the streets open up
and the canals freeze over
and the rooftops get ready
and the backyards of night are lighting up
and the parks are wide and wide open
and the empty bars are turning up the music
and the abandoned buildings, all dressed up like us,
are broken into and lit up like New Year's fireworks in Iceland.

Will you still dance
when no one needs to dance with you?

Lightning is striking somewhere, all the time.
Wait for it to roll the horizon.
Feel your bones ready for the light to burst.
Bones will be all you are.

May your radios be too loud.
May you lose your voice singing the road trip eternal.
May you let it all out.
May you stand fast in the crushing storm when there is no shelter.
May you challenge the heavens.
May you dance on the wreckage after dismantling the myth of constant hell.
May you dance the jaws of life.

Great power comes at weird times in the strangest places.
Winston Churchill was born in a woman's bathroom
during a dance.
May you enjoy the courtship
and hail its arrival.

May you make yourself big
when facing the awakened bear of your fears.
May you dance the dance of the unknown.
May you get the hell out.
May your heat melt all the sand
to make us see us.
May your heart move you so wild
your love
scars your legs."

AND THE SHAVING CREAM GOES EVERYWHERE...

for Michael Carbonaro

New Year's alone is frosting without cake
when all you want is cake.
Look out over the city of broken lamps.
You can't go to a parade alone. It's suspicious.
All mommies keep their kids close
when a single dude with a balloon looks at peace.
It's just another New Year's morning, or Tuesday.
This morning is a bad rebranding
of all vanilla mornings.

Motorized tie-rack!

Where's your shoes? The good ones?
Where's your shirt, the one that says you care?
The clean, expensive one?
Where did you place the GPS coordinates of your only dream?
Whose towel is this?

Shave your face every dog-ass day. It's
always the same. Work face. Moisturize. For what?
Are we in drier times? Look at you.
Is this your start? You fit groundhog.
Where did your madness go?

Refrigerator with a clear door!

You are everything lame you breathed out last year.
Every slow night safe. Every solo frozen dinner song.
You didn't do much last year. That's the way you like it.
Is there anything sadder
than electronic chess? If last year was a photo album,
there would be 100 photos of diet frozen yogurt.

The Gerber daisy was supposed to cheer you up,
but somehow it is brown.
The weeping fig was too spot-on.
The spider plant was supposed to be hard to kill.
It is trying to hang on like a middle-aged cheerleader's smile.

You don't have to live like you're all done.
You are what you dreamt!
Queen of the creeps! Whiskey demon! Banana bread hellcat!

You talk too much of the thing you used to be.
The heart.
Your heart is a collapsed cave.
The news on your watch said there were survivors.

Look at you. You don't even appear the same.
You lost weight but not the burden.
Your lover took the TV and left you
skin and bones. Dogs drool over
your last days.

I'm a good boy! Gimme them big human bones!

Lover, was I too much? Too damn sincere?
I don't want to be what I have been.
I want someone to notice that I use recycled bags now.
I want the sleek mystery of the wanted, the gorgeous other.
I want to be my true self and not be scared of strangers.

I'm tired of this long joke of an exhale.
I want my head untucked and my good blood out.
I will be dignified from now on.

Or not! Banana Bread Man lives!

What are you?
Clean madness, the cutlery of madness, the purest
mess.

Oh, God.
I forgot to shave.
I've just been playing with the shaving cream.
Look at you.
I missed you.
Covered in what looks like too much frosting.

You need cake!

Welcome back.
You must get to know the madness
for the madness is bright.

I speak the command into my phone,
'Give me Madness! Give it raw!'
But all that comes
is the sound of ska.

SWALLOW THE HOUSE

who are you?
swallow the house.
who are you?
throw up the chimney.
who are you?
darkness ain't all that.
who are you?
throat forced closed in the living room.
who are you?
wet books. You felt too much.
who are you?
the one noticing what all these new shoes mean
at the wake.

TEXAS ON A
SATURDAY NIGHT

WRITE BLOODY TACTICAL MANUALS
EST. 2004

ELEGANCE

Matt was at peace with his drink, a speed metal looking dude with a kind face, quiet and cool next to me at the American Legion Hall.

How did you end up in Elgin, Texas?

I dunno. It's a long story.

I'm listening.

I mean, I know, but it's too long.

Let's drink these, and then you can tell as much as the beer will allow.

I was living in Queens. Married. Working at Kinko's.
Everything sucked. My job. My marriage. My tiny, expensive apartment.
I felt heavy and just went walking after work.
I didn't stop walking.

The next day
the cops found me 'cause my wife said I had lost my mind. They
asked me questions and were sure I had lost my mind. I tried to tell them I just
needed to keep walking. They put me in an ambulance. Drove me to the hospital
entrance. I was sitting in that ambulance back
there, alone. I just got out when it stopped and ran, caught a cab to LaGuardia.
I only knew one thing. I wanted one thing and nothing else.
I wanted to see the St. Louis Cardinals play.

I drained my bank account and flew that day to St. Louis. Sitting in
that stadium at night, I finally felt good. Then I realized I didn't have a step two.

I called my parents,
and they didn't yell at me.
They wanted to know what I was going to do next.
I told them I didn't know.

I said I finally did the one thing I wanted to do and I feel good and
I can't go back to that old life. I can't touch any of it.
They said they knew of some jobs in Elgin, Texas.
Now, here I am. Single. Bartending. Tiny, cheap apartment here, but
it's fine. I feel fine now.

Does that make me sound crazy?

It makes you sound like the best.

Change of pace is good. Sometimes somewhere else is all you need.

I don't know if that's true. I still don't think I know what I need. I think I'm pretty good,
though, at seeing what I don't need. That's somethin'. What were you trying to get away
from that brought you here to Elgin?

I wasn't trying to get away from anything. Wait. That's a good question.
Is trying to find something the same as trying to get away from something?

I dunno. It's hard to be honest when you're thirsty. You're not gonna write about this, are ya?

Nope. I don't really see the poetry in it.

JOHNNY CASH AND THE SAD TROMBONE

You're right, Willie.
There is nothing quite like Texas on a Saturday night.
Here lies our range life, more space than pavement,
land of grand escape, our traffic
banishment, and fresh tomato gloat fest.
Heart skips a beat when she wears an Elgin Wildcat ball cap,
summoning deadly sunlight and afternoon winds that try
to whip her ponytail.

At the Liberty Tree pub, she pulls up her anchor in the sea of heartbreak.
Lucinda is shooting God and gravel from the speakers.
See how the cowgirls honk their tonk?
Her limbs drink the sway of Indian Paintbrush.

The heart wants what it wants,
and it wants mutton busting and hoop earrings.
Return to this twang of a love song. Goodbye, empty caress.
Hello, fields of Coastal Bermuda that have seen so many fade and arrive.

I take a job DJ'ing on Saturdays.

I accidentally hit the Sad Trombone sound effect
in the middle of Johnny Cash's version of Jackson.
"We got married in a fever" wah wah wah—
The whole bar turning to me, most of 'em laughing,
wondering what I was
trying to imply.

I took to the mic and said,
"It's Saturday night! I don't really know what I'm doing."

I look at you at the bar, laughing harder than anyone else,
and this smile is a truth
as wide as the great state itself.

YOU GOTTA MEAN BUSINESS

Living in the wide-open prairie of Elgin, Texas, I asked the clerk at the Do It Best hardware shop if they had any bug tasers.

Oh, you mean bug zappers. Yes, these'll draw insects from a one acre radius.

No, sir. You don't understand. I don't want to hurt anyone. I want to show the bugs I mean business, but I don't want to kill them.

But if you don't kill them, they won't think you mean business.

So they'll tell the others that I showed too much mercy?

Exactly. You kill some and the rest are empowered at first for revenge, but revenge doesn't last.

In some.

True, in some.

ALL HAIL THE KINDNESS OF STRANGERS

What about all the friendly racists?
How will you deal with people not agreeing with you?
Are you gonna get a gun, a six pack of God, and a pickup truck?
Will it be weird not living around Asians?
Are you ready for the sun to kick your candy ass everyday?
How will you handle it when the lady at the DMV asks your profession,
and you try to tell her "full-time poet," but she doesn't understand,
so she just stamps your application with the word
Pussy?

I only know this:
I moved here to Texas, where my father was born and raised, several years ago.

The clerk at Target in North Austin saw my hands full and ran to get
me a cart without asking.

A bartender named Topaz at the Sahara Lounge asked if we were new in town.
I sheepishly said, *Yes, like everyone else.*
He said, *Welcome home,* and I felt the murder of love in whiskey.

A waitress winked at me when I got a ringer playing washers
in the open air of Contigo.
It wasn't flirty. It said, look at you, you did something good.
I knew you could do it.

The bartender at the American Legion in Elgin, Texas,
noticed tear streaks drying on my girlfriend's face
and asked if she could give her a hug.
My girl said It's okay. I just dropped my Mom off at the airport. It's alright.
The bartender came around the bar to her stool and hugged her anyway.

The past is all cast away and frosted glass.
Home is a feeling.
All hail the kindness of strangers.
You can handle the weather anywhere if there are good people.

Maybe too much good weather makes great people bad.
Maybe bad weather
makes it feel like
we made it through something, together.

To my friends in the West:
I have found there's good and bad everywhere you go.

Maybe everyone is nice in Texas
because it's so easy to shoot someone in the face
if they're not nice.

Oh, and
I own two guns now.
You gotta come visit.

BAR HOP WRITING EXERCISE GONE WRONG

Eric is so horny
I can smell the pineapple pulp
fruiting up his sperm.

A fella, alone at the table next to us, texts someone all night,
and you can tell from the thumb intensity
that they will never show up.

At the Jackalope, I feel like fresh bread.
I tell this to Eric.
"Your legs feel like fresh bread?"
No, Eric. I want some fresh bread.
"Fresh bread? You mean new poon?"
No. I'm in the mood for fresh bread.
'I do not know what the fuck you mean.'
I forgot he was in poetry mode and I was just hungry.
I decided to play along when he asked,
'What do you mean, fresh bread? Who is fresh bread?'
Dammit, Eric! Look inside yourself. Look!

A young, cute dorm-ish woman
finally comes along to hit on Eric.
She says, "Sir. Could I borrow your cell phone
to call my Ma. She is going to pick us up, and mine is dead."
He and I feel our skin begin to Clint Eastwood
at the word *sir,*
and he tells her *Heeeeeell* no
like a weirdo.

The bachelorette party across from us, wearing New Orleans
wrong, asks us what we are writing.

We tell them poetry.
They ask us why.
The question, it is
what is wrong
with everything.

GIRL PIZZA AT BACKSPACE IN AUSTIN

Her dress is blooming.
My beer is shore break.
All things full and loving
in a charcuterie.

No one knows you when you're sober.

No one knows you
when you're too shy to say
hello.

The walls are blank.
No art makes me hungry.

Steal the glance.
She changes the air.

I love seeing beauty,
but I hate learning someone.

Does the exhaustion of new people
keep us married?

Your dress is great.
'I know. I only wear great dresses.'

I smile, bail without doing the 'bad film look-back'
and enjoy the long feeling
of going nowhere.

THE POET
VS.

TOO MANY DRINK TICKETS

WRITE BLOODY TACTICAL MANUALS
EST. 2004

SOUR MASH

and so you hit the road with some other white poets
and you washed diner dishes in Dallas for a discount on your meal
and they passed the hat around the audience
and you made 50 bucks
and you bought everyone pancakes at Norm's
and years later you hit the road alone
and they paid you 200 bucks
and you bought yourself a dozen loseable sunglasses
and a flask to make it through the open mic
and then you hit the road
with a queer author and a black dude
and they paid you 1500 each.

and you knew you could make a go of this poetry thing
that sucked at your chicken legs and made you follow
and you saw yourself changed
and you thought this kind of art form
could be medicine
and not just embalming fluid.

and you and the power blonde
put on shows in aquariums
and the audience loved it
but they didn't buy much
and you only sold two shirts and three books
and you tried going big and began opening up for rock bands and comics
and you learned that dancing and laughing
had a higher market value than metaphor
and you took the gigs, all the gigs as the gorgeous talked through your sets
and licked the love in their phones
and you took the job reading your work at the party clubs
and read to a room that mingled around the images that broke your ass
and your stack of ideas sold nothing as someone told you
that you were great ambience.
Ugh. You never wanted to be ambience.

and you applied for the grants
and wondered what you'd get to do
if you
won them all,
but you lost them all
and didn't know most of the words in
the winners proposals.

and the publisher
thought you were sexist
because you wrote the poem
about eavesdropping
on your ex-girl during her date
after seeing her car parked outside the bar
and as she spoke low of you, you hot crawfished
and you were the creep that just listened
like a scene from Mannequin 2
and couldn't wait to write down the poison that kept yelling like
a dog locked inside a four-door summer
and the publisher tried to teach
you that real life sells, unless it's needy
and is often too offensive to sell books
and to go learn the truth
that makes people cheer.

the truth between strangers:

the weather.
listen to how we feel about the weather.
write about the moon
but not about how it fucks up our blood.

and no one wanted to
risk their book sales
by talking about what we all
talked about at the bar.

you all lied to the interviewer when she said:
have you ever had a racist thought?

have you ever had a million thoughts at once?
have you ever wanted to murder someone?
have you ever realized you were lying about love?
have you ever wanted to die because of how you used to be/are?
have you spent more time writing about living than doing it?

and some of you and your friends got so turned on
by the hunt for evil people, the detestable, the black energy of losers,
you stayed erect for days
and wrote 'everyone is wrong'
with your gleaming cocks and perfect nipple ink.

and some of your friends realized that loneliness was power
and they slipped away.

and some of you and your remaining friends
kept writing inspirational
'hang in there' pieces
cause the rest was too hard to live off of
and the nasty was making us lose fans
and we didn't write anything broken, fuck-heavy, cheap or dirty anymore
and we justified it because we really wanted this one bastard art form
to reach the masses and change the world, or at least a township
because we thought it was better,
we knew a great line of poetry was a bullet and novels were a long choke
and no one had time anyway for real phone calls or involved dinners
so we nailed the fast power of today by turning to poetry
but we poets only argued online amongst ourselves
and pretended that it mattered.

we glowed like we could change the world from an anonymous laptop.

the reviews came in:
your poetry didn't change anything—
it just moved the monster
to the other side of the room.

you thought about real estate sales and finally eating well
you thought about sheep wrangling residencies where your hands become soil

you thought about being a motorcycle mechanic
that actually fixes something—

anything to feel real and stop wondering
about capturing the 'you don't know what.'

to fuck when you want to and not
ponder the beauty.
to drink when you need to
and not unlock the diary.
to wander in the woods and not
look through the pines
for a great closing line.

to have an internal fuck you every time
you look at trees and say
yes, they are beautiful...but they are wet and living.
what does that mean?

morning dew aint day tears
storms are not angel farts,
cum is not the dying, drying frost of love.

you used to think poetry was important only to poets,
and now you know that isn't true.

poetry is important to few poets
is true,
as you loom in the libraries of your fellow writers
and notice that if they own more than 10 poetry books
almost everyone is dead.

writers have a hard time
loving now. So, go.

close it all down.
close it all down   .
and finish the applications.

then, you get a letter.
someone says they *needed*
one of the poems you wrote.
not that they liked it. needed it.
you try to laugh it off. You try to say you are making
a little lost thing important. The way the bones of your child
found in a lake can be seen as sticks if you don't know.
you try to see something cynical
in how you feel reading the letter.

but all that comes now is
you feel like taking out the trash
and even though you don't know how to—
you want to skip around like an idiot

the great amnesia sets in. and it's back to—

hello, blue bonnets swaying across wide Texas.
hello, all you animals flying above in the blue, blue laundry.
hello to the quiet someone
who removes darts
from the other side of night
and leaves us with
the many little holes
of surprise light.

LIBERATION BLUES

Of course, the French waiter was skinny—he was French.
He had a slight Aussie/Parisian accent, which is a strange soup, but
Canberra is home to the strange and the new.

The American-sounding blues band kept playing after my reading,
nailing SRV into the lobby walls.

Of course, I was exhausted and wanted to loosen the feeling that
comes after you shake too many post-show hands to feel sincere.
Of course, I wanted more Tasmanian whiskey and an Aussie Rules
Football match in my room to unwind alone.

Of course, the Frenchie came up to me and asked if he could give me
a hug.
Some fans do this, and there is either a true sweetness or it feels like a dare.
Of course, I thought him to be a chiseled drunk. He looked like a spy.
And he was French.

I asked him why he wanted a hug.
He asked if it was true, if I was in the 82nd Airborne. I said yes, in the '90s.
He said his grandfather lived in a village in the north of France
liberated by the 82nd during WWII and that his grandfather said if
he ever met an American paratrooper to give them a hug because if
not for them, he would not be here, nor his father, nor him. He held
out his arms and said, so thank you for, in a way, letting me be here.

Of course, I hugged him and told him I didn't do anything.
He said I was the first American Paratrooper he'd ever met, so it still meant a
lot to get to say thank you.
Of course, his eyes welled up.
Of course, I was ashamed that I didn't feel anything.

Of course, we shook hands post-hug, and I packed up my gear.
Of course, I went out alone
and got hammered on beer and strolled, blasted silly,
until I ran out of the colorful cash
and felt nothing.

I listened to the music playing over the lake
and felt nothing.

Of course, when it all wore off,
I looked up into the night air
and looked as far as I could
and cried like a lost child.

FAVORITE ROLLER DERBY NAMES I MADE UP IN PORTLAND AT Claudias BAR WHILE ON TOUR; UNCLAIMED SO FAR

for Juliet and The Rose City Rollers

cruela da skill

queen elizabitch

rink witherspoon

princess slaya

crash bandikooch

miss guided missle

gatorbabe

brasby skills and bash

barbrahamber tamblyn

mary tyler morgue

mc jammer

boobie howser, m.d.

florence henderscum

family splatters

aborshauna

boob marley

Lisa

ANOTHER PROBLEM WITH POETRY

Billy Collins grew tired of poets
assigning precious light to the day,
telling us that they spotted a bird
and were now confident
that beaks were a gentle religion.

And the poets surrounded Billy at the book signing
and asked him,
"How wet can seaweed really get? Really."
And then they asked how wet seaweed could get
on the inside of itself, begging him to write about this,
how he could magically link it to
how our blood goes dry when tainted by air
and how tainty the daylight when death awakes!
And how love is seaweed reaching fast to daylight
and make us see that *we be seaweed*,
make us see that we are special Billy! Do your job!

But Billy stands and says,
quiet please.
Seaweed
has never been in love
and wasn't designed for it
and seaweed musings
will never help you put food on the table
unless you are me or what you wished me to be.

Billy sits. Does a Kegel. Stands again and says,
Real quiet, please—revision!
Now, some seaweeds live with the sole purpose of
choking out other native forms
which starves other marine life until there is only death.

I, too, am here for great coffee, fancy sex, and then I choke. That's it.

Billy takes a deep breath,
asks for super quiet, says,
Remember this: in Wales they make Laver bread from seaweed.
In Japan, sheets of it nourish for sushi.
In Belize, sweet milk.
It heals the face in the United States.

And then he screams.

Billy ends the night yelling one note at the top of his lungs
for several minutes
and they still burst into applause
and he realizes for the first time
as he signs some guys breast
that his handwriting is beautiful
without having to make it
sound that way.

THE YAWNER IN THE BACK OF THE VENUE, ROLLED EYES, THE EDUCATED SMILE, THE NUDGED RIBS, THE SENTIMENTALITY; SENTIMENTALITÉ AND MELODRAMA PUSS, LENDER OF LEFT HOOK, A SOFTNESS; ZACHTHEID! AND OUR WILLINGNESS TO BE SUCKERED

Naomi was bored by poetry
but still went to the readings
at the Rosenau to watch her friends'
attempts at "filleting" their emotions.

Derrick, would you and Joel like to come to a house party?

We would love to.

Okay, but no talk of poetry.
I don't want everyone to kill themselves.

After drinking to the point where we sang
Springsteen in high heels,
someone suggested we hike into the hills
overlooking the city.

When the others got out of site,
Naomi, the tall, gorgeous, disinterested one
who seemed more like a mistrusting nurse,
slammed me into the wooden fence,
smacked me hard across the face like an old-timey duel
and kissed me. She kept doing it,
fighting to get her hands free as I struggled to clench them down,

as if each smack would be soothed with a harder kiss.
It was bizarre, fantastic, and super German.
It was the strangest payback
for world war II.
I loved her throw-pillow lips.

I'd like to see her again, just to catch up over a shandy.
Are you married now, Naomi?
I can imagine looking around the bar
for the fella with the most blood pouring out of his face.

I can't forget
lying in the dirt
covered in sunrise,
wanting to move there,
live a life where I had to tell strangers daily,
"Um. I fell."

5:30 A.M. is always a story.

Wine sent us into the darkness.
We talked about the future.
Nothing much came of it.

Beautiful correction.

Wir befaßten uns der mit Zukunft.
Wein sendete uns in die Schwärzung.
Nichts kam von ihm.

SHORT POEMS REJECTED BY HIGHLIGHTS MAGAZINE

What's the Pope's
favorite body part?

The umbiblical cord.

What's the fittest but
scariest monster of all time?

The abdominal snowman.

What makes a Shaman
feel left out?

When rappers make it rain.

THE WANDERING HOW

Green easy,
hunching hills of Germany.
Blue glass,
glacial jags of Austria.
Snow slushed,
streets holding out for curd gravy in Vancouver.
Tight bridges,
lost on Campari and midnight Averna, rolling over tight bridges of Venice, Italy.
Stubborn tundra,
sled husky's with A.D.D., pissing while running, racing over virgin Alaska.
Jarred fireflies,
the grocery on home street in Atlanta where the music is fresh-power and hollering.
Autumn crisp,
kids napping safe in leaf piles near Dartmouth.

I am home.

Sweetness awaits,
open arms of non-war, foreign beds, dinner parties ready to listen,
a freeing love in the arms of strangers, to share darkness
and not bloat.

The right feeling when it is time to get gone.
How non lost at sea lost can feel,
How non mugger hungry the dirty ones smile,
How non failed at school defining we can become,
How non clunked steady by the golf clubs of love,
How non crushed by the empty air of 'what if I still suck,"
the waiting world really is.

A rucksack full of grit,
a heart compressed in a hostel bunk,
the tone of voice coming from a locket,
told you to keep pushing up the hill. Was it Kate Bush?
No matter how broke, how jib flipped, how outscored,
how hungry you get–

you kept wanting to impress your Mother.
Thank you is un-poetic.
Thank you.

MENDER/DESTROYER
for COA

Cristin and I were chatting
about her breakup, her new life
how everything was brand new
and then—

    her chair broke,
and she fell to the floor
like mashed potatoes.

She didn't cry.
She just laid there, stretched out
and looked like an extra waiting
for action to be called in a catastrophe film.

When a poet eats it, they begin sorting out the meaning
of all broken chairs,
of all support
surprising you
and caving in suddenly,
unsure of
what sucks more—the bruise or
having to check chairs for the rest of your life.

I helped her up. Swung open the glass door.
I threw the chair high into the backyard air
and watched it shatter.

"Fuck this chair.
This chair is from the forest of assholes.
This chair can eat my hot fuck and die."

Cristin then quietly went outside barefoot,
collected the pieces from the grass,
and took it into the garage
so she could fix it.

"It didn't break.
I broke it."

POEM FOR WEEDS TAVERN, CHICAGO

"Aw, man! I'm sick of (Weird pause)
wishing on stars!
I want the stars (Weirder pause)
to wish
upon me, (Vocal fry) America!
(Pretend to almost cry)
I can't tell
if our flag is still waving (Now get whispery)
or if it's just
waving
(As if it just came to you)
goodbye…"

MR. MARKS

I was hosting a book release party
for The Good Things About America
in a massive theatre in Santa Ana, and there in the audience
sat Mr. Marks, my high school drama teacher.

We didn't even sell 100 tickets for the 500 seat theatre.
I could see everyone's face
as they had all
kindly moved
toward the front of the house.

22 years after our class together, Mr. Marks sat
with his wife in the front row.
I always daydreamed in the back of his class
but remembered loving his easy style.
I recognized his face as I announced the next poet
and had never been so nervous in all my life.

Backstage, I fantasize about him coming up to me with a medal saying,
"You were trouble, Derrick, but I knew
you'd make it at something. I could see the gold flints of genius in
your eyes at such a young age. You didn't deserve those bad grades.
On behalf of Pacifica High School, take this necklace thingy."

I came out into the audience after the show.
I reached out to shake his hand,
but he and his wife Patty
surrounded me in a hug. They said
they were proud of me.
They said, 'who knew you'd be a successful poet?'

As they left up the aisle towards the exits,
I looked at the stacks of hundreds of books at the merch table
that we didn't sell.
I thought of the retainer we didn't cover for the theatre
and the debt for paying the band,

the overwhelming anchor falling feeling that
I, once again, didn't do something right
to fill the seats.

Mr. Marks had turned at the top of the aisle
and walked towards me.
He held the book up and said,
"I almost forgot to have you sign my copy."

I told him I was sorry about the show,
that it has gone much better in the past
and sorry for the strange energy and empty house.

He said, "What the hell are you talking about?
You got almost 100 people to come out and hear some poetry.
I am very impressed. We thought we would be some of the
only ones here."

He gave me one last hug, the good kind,
where you hold the shoulders after to sturdy them.
It put helium in my chin.

I noticed that, for no reason,
I had been trying to hide my beer from him
behind my leg
the entire time.

NICE PAINKILLERS, STAY HAUNTED

Everyone in Berlin is tired from fucking.
Kreuzberg.
George Strait is cooling every juke.
Proud dogs shit in Nazi watchtowers.
Lovers trying English on.
A city beaten with bats, the graffiti
coming back to its cheeks.
Why are these glasses of beer so small?
What's the rush?
Gray before God and McDonald's,
Gray after.
How oppression and grief
let some places grow into a garden
where the creatives
dump their hearts and make the dead lands useful
while some places that don't lure the wild just stay haunted.
Music from the park.
Chess.
River drunk.
I notice the plaque on the sidewalk,
(which, at first, I think is just a historical marker,)
notes the Jew
who had this building stolen
from him and his family
and was sent off to die.
I buy painkillers in the
Apoteka and notice it.
I notice them everywhere now.
Little gold tombstones
on your way
to the club.

SCIENTIFIC AMERICAN

Every time a poet
uses the word
'soul'
hell expands,
just enough.

MISPLACED COMPLIMENTS

I've been trying to live a more positive life.
Last year I lived on a boat in Long Beach called the Sea Section,
and when I passed some grizzled fishermen, I'd yell,
"What'd ya catch!"
And they'd say, "Nothin'!"
And I'd say, "Well, catch this compliment: you're beautiful!"

DARKNESS,

EARLY TO THE PARTY

WRITE BLOODY TACTICAL MANUALS
EST. 2004

TONGUE ON THE WALL

"No one should outlive his power." -John Davidson

Being forgotten is not as bad
as hoping you aren't.

A bridge crosses the Mississippi.
Berryman stands upon it.
The bells spoke.
Feet first.
Beard flipping up
like a tent flap in the breeze.
Jumps.
Misses the water.
Hits the bank.

Hard earth is less scary than dark, forgiving rivers?

Because the soil could push out
what you couldn't?

I write in a library of a dead poet,
a remodeled home in Lenox, Massachusetts
and I don't know any of the titles on the white shelves.

I feel dumb
as last week when I saw
the first book I ever wrote
in a used bookstore
for a dollar.

I wanted to cry. I tried so hard. All these books
tried so hard.

Now I want to stop, not because someone
abandoned my work, but because
there is just so much
and it really ain't nothin'.

Someone kissed me once and bruised me good and it ain't enough,
and I know what a snowmobile feels like in mid-air and it ain't enough,
and I got lost in sunlight on an island and found unopened wine and it ain't
      enough.

I have a couple of good dream songs that are my best
and it ain't nothin'.

John Berryman's Dad,
shotgun blasting his tongue onto the wood paneling,
how that photo repeated on every page of Berryman's books,
the end of language,
the end of Boy.

John are you whispering:
you just don't know.
You just don't know
yet.

Poetry didn't take your life.
It kept you here.

It kept you here until you closed your eyes
to the spirits from smokestacks, to the lawns of America
and grew away from the power of swallowing song-birds
and the hissing fuels of night. You turned away.
Not us.

Did going inside kill you?
I hope you missed the river on purpose.

If you dig at a foundation for too long
the home
will collapse.

John, John, over-read John.

Being forgotten is not as bad
as hoping you aren't.
We hear you every day

and shove you back down.
Stillness,
stillness
ain't nothin'.

THEY LOVED YOU, BUT YOU TELEGRAPHED TOO MUCH
A broken sestina.

We are all in the same hotel, finally at once.
No one can remember the sky. All Black pulp.
No one knows how they got here.
This hotel feels like loose air, like an airplane that is never cleared to land.
There is plenty of room for all of us, in the black.
At this hotel, no one comes to help you with your fat bags.
You fat bag.
The walls lined with chicken factory feathers. Nothing echoes.

All hail the quiet yellow rooms of the three star hotel
and the empty sound of a complimentary coffee mug catching blops of whiskey.
All hail the hot knock of sunlight and comforters that ruffle with stiff disease. So
sudden, the tiny shampoo won't be enough to get you clean. The curved shower
curtain rods can't
keep away Feeling
and there is no art on any wall to love.
Lay out your clothes in a disaster. Is anyone coming for you? Is he in a robe?
How hard you have worked to make yourself so unfuckable.

Have you ever seen anyone win a fight in a robe?
Have you ever seen a writer inferno a whole hotel
just by drunkenly over-magnifying the day, roasting the ants of love?
Have you ever seen a dancer that breaks the day they realize they have always
been dancing alone?
The thing waits in you, the thing Dylan Thomas could not kill with whiskey
or light. Rage, rage into the dying of the wallpaper and cheap breakfast. The
remote control is a feeling,
so you wait for it to come to you and teach you of change, power, and something
sudden from the black.

Why won't you roam the lobby in the robe
and save someone? Save them from destination brochures and feeling.
Did you build this hotel?

One star hotel means no one cares, means dirty freedom, means low budget felony love.
Two stars means sleep will come at you like a sudden
black wind. Save money on the room so you can afford better whiskey. Her name was light.

Her name was service. Her name was wet and hard as fuck. Her name
wanted me to bite her
shoulder. Her name crawled around me like a snow rescue. Her name
tightens in my mouth.
Better whiskey means better dreams, black pulp.
Three star hotels should mean
someone comes to ask you if you need any help carrying any of that 49 pound feeling.
Lift.

It was 56, but the airlines made you get it down to a 49 pound kind of feeling
or they charge you.

You just wanted to get to the highest room of the hotel
and feel all the people stacked beneath you, wanting to feel something sudden
in their chest. From the closet hanger, they all remove the bath robe
and lay on it, wrapping the sleeves around them, wanting to be touched by
an animal full of blood, unable to speak of their loneliness. Open mouths.
Black pulp.

We are a crowd of unshared whiskey.
We are the hotel that has remodeled over the feeling.
We are lying on large beds, embraced in the sleeves of an empty robe.
Suddenly, housekeeping/sunlight will knock through every room of the yellow hotel.

Fill the mug with whiskey, open the windows and wait for love—
you swallow darkness until it swallows you.
You must eat it all to grow sick of it.
Night comes and the lobby fills with people in robes, and no one knows how
to say that one thing.

CAKE WEEK

She laid across the grave trying to hug it, trying to will herself into the ground.

I couldn't believe it still broke her up this hard after so many years.

When someone visits the grave of a loved one, and you don't know what to do because you didn't know the deceased,
you look around to see if your name is on any tombstone. You try to show sympathy.

You hold her and try to tell her that we love the spirit and not the flesh. Their spirit is always around us.

She will tell you that you are wrong.

Both, Derrick. Both. It's like a painting. We don't love Matisse's paints.
We do love what we saw, what we held, and we can also be amused by how it got there.
The spirit is just paint. I don't get much from photographs. You would always
rather go to the museum to see a painting rather than in a book. It might
make me feel good to say I loved their spirit, but I love both. I loved his
woodshop hands. I loved his chipped tooth and skin that looked pulled down by
the weights in the air. I can miss what I can't see anymore.

What a fucking joke that we have to go away.

It's like giving someone coconut cake
and it becomes their favorite thing
and then someone says you can only have it
for a week
and then never again.

Yeah, but how good
is that week
of cake?

YOU WILL BE DESTROYED IN YOUR OWN WAY

All the pictures I tried to take were too sudden
and poorly framed.
Half-faced soldiers.
Blurry telephone poles.
Too much ceiling, not enough body.

I'm 18 and don't know how to plan a shot.
I feel a thing, and I grab the thing
that captures the thing
and shoot.
You must be quick on the draw
because everything goes away
so fast.
I shoot with confidence and
confidence is nothing recognizable,
nothing is recognizable.

I'm constantly making the world's worst film:
young men in green, same haircut,
loaded down with the loneliness
of dying towns.
The world won't remember their names.
Me neither.

They are going through the tear gas chamber today.
You have to take it all in.
You have to let it destroy some of you
so you can have confidence.
There is no other way.

No one wants to be the guy who can't control the snot,
how it flushes flood, gushes like a storm well.
No one wants to be the guy who pisses himself
crawling under M60 tracers.
No one wants to be trembling clumsy at the grenade training,

throwing a pin down range
and blowing your and the Drill Sergeant's legs off.
No one wants to be the God who believes we would all make it,
the guy who cries when the mail doesn't come.
You wanna be a man,
but you got no blueprint.

Here at the chemical weapons shacks,
the gas gets us all in some manner.

Remove your mask, and yell your battery's motto:

"Mad Dogs, Mad Dogs, we got guts! Mad Dogs, Mad Dogs, we kick butts!
1st platoon, second to none, if we can't do it, it can't be done!
Drive on, Drill Sergeant, drive on! Travel on, Drill Sergeant, drive on!
Dogs—YO!—Hit 'em hard! Woof woof woof!"

We stand in the yellow smoke,
remove our chemical masks,
and take it in, the hot mustardy, mace juice
so we know what it's like
when war ruins the air.

Everyone waits by the exit door, heckling the afflicted,
waiting to see how the gas affects each Private.

Some itch. Some cry madly. Some foam at the mouth.
Some cheer and gag. Some claw at their eyes. Some
flow uncontrollably from the nose and cack cack.

We lived.
We laughed at each other's suffering.
It was okay.

I fell asleep that night and felt burnt inside.
Not the CS gas.
I missed someone and didn't know who.
I thought all of my soot and anger
would soak up someone's clean heat by now.

I thought I would look good in a uniform
and someone would see me as a man
they could trust.

A wet, canvas tent has a smell that is lonely.
Soldiers are the opposite of poetry.
Drivers of death.
Death is not that different than
waiting on someone to want you.

Looking out towards the long woods,
I watch the hummingbirds, wings a-blur.
Just a blur moving them around.

I look at old photos
and wish I was better.

FIELD MANUAL ON HOW TO USE THE LATRINE WHILE WEARING MOPP 4 CHEMICAL PROTECTIVE GEAR

1. Avoid Low Areas and Areas with Heavy Brush.

You can easily be spotted squatting from a low level position.
Heavy brush makes heavy noise. It gives you away.

2. Provide Security. If Possible, Have a Buddy Go with You.

Have a buddy go with you that does not mind being quiet while you are in your mode.
Have a buddy go with you that is not prone to laughing while you are in your mode.
Laughing can get you killed.
Have a buddy go with you only if your buddy agrees to defend you when you are defenseless.
Most will go alone.

3. Scrape Away At Least 2 Inches of Surface Area with Your Entrenching Tool.

This is so you have a place for your weapon to rest.
How often your weapon rests will always be up to you.

4. The Area Shold Be Large Enough to Hold Your Weapon and Your Load Carrying Euipment (LCE).

Dig a hole one-foot deep.
This may not seem deep enough to hold all your shit,

but, trust me, this is all the room you need.

5. **Keep Your Weapon Within Arms Reach.**

Can you imagine having to shoot someone while
relieving yourself?
Can you imagine living a life
where one burden that you couldn't wait to
release finally goes away
and the next burden is that
you murdered someone... in a weird way? In an amazing way!

6. **Keep Your Armored Vest and Helmet on.**

It may seem more comfortable, but a bullet in
the heart is verifiably
less comfortable,
unless the bullet is symbolic.

7. **Remove Packets from the Skin Contamination Kit.**

8. **Decontaminate Your Gloves.**

9. **Pull Up the Over Garment Jacket by Grasping
the Bottom of the Jacket and Folding It Back
on Itself, and Open the Trousers.**

Decontaminate your gloves again if necessary.
Unsnap and unzip the trousers.
What do you see?
Is it the reason?

Peel the trousers down from your body to
perform the specific function.
You are the most dangerous banana.
When I say perform the specific function,
please keep it specific.

10. Remove Your Protective Gloves Carefully.

11. Do Not Touch a Contaminated Area on the Outer Garment.

Who knows where you have been?
Who knows where you have been?

12. Unbutton Your Battle Dress Uniform and Pull Down Your Trousers.

13. Lower Your Underwear And Eliminate the Waste from Your Body.

One of these steps out of order is humiliating and draws bugs.

14. Use the M25881 Skin Decontamination Kit to De-Contaminate the Skin That May Have Become Contaminated.

The Skin Decontamination Kit should never be used to contaminate the skin since it is impossible to contaminate the skin with a kit that is only used for de-contamination.

If chemical warfare in your combat area lasts for days, you may be tempted to sandbag several of these phases.
You may become angry and ask yourself:
"How did we come up with this stuff? How can we do this to each other?
How can we get back to that place where we can all shit in peace?"

No one in your unit will be allowed to skip any of the phases.

Do not enjoy each phase. Get through each phase hastily.

15. Pull up Your Underwear and Battle Dress Uniform.

16. Put Your Gloves Back On. Do Not to Touch the Outside of Your Gloves.

17. Pull Up the Over Garment.

18. Re-Secure Your Weapon.

19. Ensure All Toilet Paper and Gloves Are in the Hole.

If you look in the hole, say goodbye to that which was inside you.

It is a home.
Your home will look similar.
Deeper.

Pack down the earth and camouflage the area.
No one should know that you were ever here.

20. Continue the Mission.

SEEING BLOOD IN THE OCEAN

"Built for the arts of peace and to link the old world with the new, the Queens
challenged the fury of Hitlerism in the battle of the Atlantic. Without their aid,
the day of final victory must unquestionably have been postponed."

-Winston Churchill

Is that Emily's blood? How strange that
blood is alive. I can't wrap my head around it.
Blood is alive.

We were swimming at sea off the stern of my boat,
and somehow
she cut her leg on a screw.
As the others on deck cared for her,
I stared into the water.

I wondered what the blood would draw forth from the bottom.
I recalled that I always swim underwater with my eyes closed.

How many conquered Navies do we swim over when we
close our eyes and submerge? Imagining all the cannons
opening up, the soft bags of men, color in the foam.
To die in water and not from drowning is unfair.

I see the great tourist ship in the distance, The old Queen Mary.
Ocean after war.
Ocean after war is in us as we swim.

The Grey Ghost, The Queen Mary ship left them all to drown.
Faster than any U-boat, the speeding mammoth
had to zig-zag so she would not outrun
her protection.

She miss-timed a zig and smashed her bow
through one of her own cruiser ships, the Curacoa.
cutting the other vessel into a graveyard.

100 men, alive in the water, waving their arms
and white sailor caps
for rescue.

Horror filling their eyes as the Grey Ghost made a choice and
let them all to drown so that the 50,000 others may live.
There would be no rescue. The mission to the UK must go on.
Was it worth it?
Not when you are in the water.

Whenever someone tells me it's hard
but it's the right thing to do,
I am in the water.

Emily, I don't know how or why it works,
but the salt water
will help stop the bleeding.

THE BEST NIGHT

for Judy

"I am going to play this record very loud.
Now, let's see how you dance, knowing
that the prognosis for tomorrow
is not very good.
Dance in your exhaustion. Stay.

Stay until the night
is no longer
itself.

When you have cancer
you can't wait
for someone to come along
and make you feel
like you
finally
don't have to
go home
early."

LOUISIANA VS. THE HAIR CLUB FOR MEN

My hair quits and quits every year
and the more it quits
the less love letters you get.
It wanders
towards the silver and black
shower drain.

A lone, daddy long legs spider
slides toward the dark-
I wished him well,
cupped the water, and
dumped it on him.

Fuck you, creep.

The worst thing I saw today
was when, at the last moment,
the crook of his leg
reached up
from the hole of the drain
trying to hang on.

Oh, God. Me too, I say.
Me too.

I turned up the water
and the sliver of leg
quietly went away.

30 miles of the state of Louisiana
erodes away
every year
and there is no sorrow
to assign to it.

Me too.

IT'S FINE

The child looks like a blown safe.
The father dons his ankle chains
and clocks into the joy distillery.
The mother cleans the blood off the belt
and tries to purify the walls of the family room
with olive oil in the shape of a cross.
The child gathers his model airplane paint
to return his skin to his natural color.
The child is a blown safe.

TOODLE LOO

"We don't die, Derrick.
We take breaks from each other.
When we die,
it is a sudden break
it is a see you later. A toodle loo."

My grandfather would say this
when I asked him if he was going to die.
He hated goodbyes and insisted on all of us saying
toodle loo when leaving
because he didn't think any sad goodbye was any good.

It always felt like a tiny death to him.
Goodbye should make you feel good.
The words toodle loo tried to turn a hard moment
into something goofy.

"You gotta laugh kid. Laughter is lobster.
You can't have lobster every day.
If you did, it becomes hamburger.
You need a break from wonderful
to keep the wonderful, wonderful."

Personally, toodle loo was always way too fancy for me to say
to strangers and clerks at various shops.

"Thanks for shopping at Harley Davidson, Derrick."

Hell yeah, thanks for the new choke and chrome throttle grip. Toodle loo.

"It's not a big deal to die, Derrick.
You give up your power
if you worry about it too much.
Why give up your power?"

I couldn't go to his funeral.
I felt embarrassed
that I couldn't control
my sadness.

I wish I could have faked it.

When I get a chance to eat lobster,
especially the claw meat,
I close my eyes
and it tastes so good.

WHY MATT TAKES

OFF HIS SHIRT AT
EVERY ART GALLERY

WRITE BLOODY TACTICAL MANUALS
EST. 2004

WHAT WE LIVE WITHOUT

Stephen Wiltshire drew the ornate Royal Albert Hall following a class field trip—without the aid of a photograph. Wiltshire has the uncanny ability to draw and paint detailed landscapes and cityscapes entirely from memory. He attempted to do the same with New York City after a 20 minute helicopter ride. He drew nearly every building on the entire island to exact detail in three days, only from memory.

What curse.

He smiles like a drill team, a dentist's dream.
Stephen, staring out of the helicopter
as they miracle over New York City.
The savant is a collector,
staring at the proud concrete mess.

20 minutes in the sky
then Stephen spends three days
drawing Brooklyn, midtown to Queens,
from his clear kegs of memory.
He gets everything right.
the chunky curve of the island, the flags dying
on the bridges, the exact cars trudging gray down FDR.

What curse is the curse of precision?
To hold every memory
the way it truly was?

How we twist and bury what we saw
since we were kids
to preserve ourselves.
The greatness of kids.
Loud, pure, miniature idiots.

We hold too much in,
above ground pools bulging,
trying to not show how we are all ready
to burst at the limbs
with blood and red tenderness.

What a feeling
to recall with exactness.

I want to be as true as Stephen,
to not redirect or un-shape
or enhance what I see when I close my eyes.
To capture what is as it is.
All of it.

He recalls each chimney, window, the scale
of bridges, the stones, and glass metropolis rise.

What curse?

When I look at your New York,
I go into the lead of your seismic mind:

I see a love that can not retract.
A recollection exact.

I see your voice in your shapes, in your capture.

I see just another man, who can not let go
of a moment, flying over New York.

When I recall New York, I try as a child.
I recall the puffed throngs of zombie lords of the boulevard,
heads down, hoods up,
trudging in veils of snow; the billions of bars
flooding with whiskey and odd frenching;

the hallow porn of a crowd
of human lights
swallowing the stars.

NOT TO BE REPRODUCED

René Magritte's mother committed suicide by drowning herself in the River Sambre. This was not her first attempt at taking her own life; she had made many over a number of years, driving her husband Léopold to lock her into her bedroom. One day she escaped and was missing for days. Her body was later discovered a mile or so down the nearby river. Supposedly, when his mother was found, her dress was covering her face, an image that has been suggested as the source of several of Magritte's paintings from 1927 to 1928 of people with cloth obscuring their faces.

I am the river
Come give me your mother
I am the river
Come give me your mother

Feed this one
and surrender the other
Feed this one
and surrender the other

Send me Regina
Who longs for me so
Born in a bath
With a slight undertow

And is it so fair
This heaven and hell
That chooses us random
To howl a death knell

Leopold knows no locks can hold
A woman whose heart can shatter the cold
What can you do but be patient and kind
How the woman wields force when she's made up her mind.

I did not steal her
or send her downheart to roam
I just opened my arms
And she found her way home

The night she escaped
into my wide blue dress
she opened her mouth, singing
for my caress

Sadness is a gift
we choose to open in our blood
It will make you sing, at first a stream
but soon a flood

I am the river
Bring me your sons
I am the river
Bring everyone

Send me the ones
Who long for me so
Sing in the bath
With a slight undertow

A NIGHT OUT WITH JEFF KOONS

"Derrick, I want to hang a train from a crane."

THAT'S NOT ART, JEFF! WE ARE FUCKING DYING OUT HERE!

"Well I think life holds the highest value. You know if you remove a train from the tracks, all you hear is its breathing, the steam and breathing, the puffing. Every day it would start out, like us, breathing some, and then get up to 80 miles per hour, hanging there, and then it would slow down, until it breathed no more. Beautiful, machine, hanging there, out of steam. Like us."

Holy shit. That's beautiful.

"Schooled."

Fuck me.

"Oh, that's interesting."

SOME OF THE WILDFLOWERS

Some of the wildflowers
got caught in the combine
and the colors of bright petals
shredded in metal
found wind.

Cold yellow, brushed orange, tail feather blue confetti exploder,
all parade scattered,
coming down slow
across the one note green
of the heavy field.

The engine keeps grinding away.
The engine keeps grinding away.
The engine keeps grinding away.
The engine keeps grinding away.
The engine keeps grinding away.
The engine keeps grinding away.
The engine keeps grinding away.
The engine keeps grinding away.
The engine keeps grinding away.
The engine keeps grinding away.

So what?

The combine in New York gobbles all of these books
returned by bookstores.
Because of the glue, it cannot be recycled.
They die.

I'm sure some paper bits float up,
and a worker on the factory floor sees it,
eats his sandwich, and thinks–

I shoulda put more mustard on this.

EAT THIS SWEET CREAM, RUNT

Oh, you poor, poor people.
Waaaah! Waaaah, I'm hungry and don't have chances, waaah.
How you moan like the teak flooring of my catamaran.
You could have it so much easier
if you would only try.

The American Dream is a wet dream. You gotta get wet inside.
Flashdance bucket dump is happening inside me.

I never got help from anyone.
I delivered myself. I made my mother push with a court order.
This is how I willed myself wealthy.
I sucked my own nipples.
I saved my second wish and made my skin this color.
I ate raisins and gravel and shit out my own roads.
I drilled for oil with my marvelous dick and made my own power.
You love this rich weird dick.
I came inside myself and got a tax break; I'm family.
I deserve to not know the poor anymore.
They just want to want, chez laze, and take.
They are privileged. They get all the cool songs.
All my heroes are millionaires listening to poor folk ballads.
Gandhi was bad in bed.
Thurston Howell was a gentleman's God.

True, God gave me this ambition
to show the lazy and poor
that we are not all in this together,
that I am cream; I am a nest to look up to,
I am cream because I rose,
and they churn and churn and you may never be cream,
unless you were meant to be.
Sit the fuck down and be chaff. I lost my virginity at Sotheby's.

You think milk is expensive,
try spending 5 grand on 10 minutes of helicopter fuel.

just to get some perspective.
Fuck a Corolla.

Did you know that pre-Civil War
the word God and trust
did not used to be on our money?
Did you know it's there now?

Jesus.

ROMANCE
IS AN UNSUPERVISED
GO-CART TRACK

WRITE BLOODY TACTICAL MANUALS
EST. 2004

PLACES YOU SHOULD KISS
SOMEONE IN CALIFORNIA

1. At one of the lowest spots on earth, 227 feet below sea level,
   upon the cracked roads of that great fading accident, the once
   glitz-gone-ghost-scape of the Salton Sea. The beaches are
   skeletons, the gambling and shore fucking are gone. Last year was
   my Salton Sea.

2. At two harbors on Catalina Island. Walk to the back of the
   island, see the Pacific blanket blue sprawl, foaming, and shoulder
   shimmying, a child settling into its seat. Open your mouth and
   know the world doesn't end.

3. On the Peter Pan ride at Disneyland, gazing down at dark, busy
   London. You were almost stabbed to death in real London. You
   sprinted to the bus, and he wouldn't let you in as you screamed,
   "He is going to kill me!" The worst feeling in the world as he
   shook his head and drove off, the bike with the mugger and
   the knife racing towards you. Now, on the ride, kiss with eyes
   open and rebuild the Hackney scene, starting from the sky and
   refurbishing the night all the way down to the moving lights of
   Sunday. He is chasing you again. You are outrunning his bicycle
   still. You ran faster than you ever had and didn't want to die
   because you weren't in love. But now, you run and aren't afraid.
   He will never catch you. You are smiling. You see pirate ships
   in the air and jump. Little you is now staring at big you, in your
   flying ship, in your lap, panting, little you says, "We made it."

4. After firing a .357 revolver at the gun range in Huntington
   Beach, when you feel like artillery. Do not reverse the order. I
   will cut the mouth out of the cartoon burglar on my target and
   press my lips through the bullet holes. I know, it's a bit much.

5. 5. While doing tequila shots at the Casbah in San Diego. Tell
   them you can't remember the last good storm, a storm where
   you could feel the roof begging to give up.
   Until now.

6. At the Queen Mary's observation deck bar. Touch the teak and feel the hands of all before who couldn't imagine being gone, who held on like they would burn into this place. Kiss when your hands get hot.

7. The Antler Inn among Twin Peaks in the California mountainside, the one with the stiff Bloody Mary's and wood everything. I will kiss you hard enough to get snowed in.

8. Ask at the Santa Barbara winery, since you are advanced people, to move on straight from the wine tasting to the wine drinking. If they only pour a little, tell them we can only hydrate on the colors of blood. If they are amused and fill you up, kiss her, sloppy. Then describe the kiss pretentiously.

9. Stand upon the Ravenna Bridge late at night in the Canals of Naples, California. Watch for the drunks trying to screw in the passing gondolas. When you hear Santa Lucia, kiss, and feel like happy hour at Crow's is upon you.

10. I miss you. I ran outta poetry.

11. I knew you would read this. I am trying to trick you into thinking I always think this way. Kiss me while the college girls dance around us at The Short Stop in Echo Park. Skirts flush with lust and low GPA's, pounding the floor into new dust, stomping their mark into the yearbook of the floor. We were here. We danced around these two idiots that couldn't stop making out.

12. Deep in The Magic Castle, the recessed room within the cliff, the close up rooms, and write down the hardest thing you ever went through. Let me guess it. Kiss as my fingers go across the deep pencil lines. How am I always right? Only the dead hearted bastard tries to figure it all out.

13. Get on the back of my motorcycle down PCH and smell: strawberry fields, sage, jet fuel. Smell what you've been missing. Kiss me up the 101 when 70 mph feels like home. Home. It's a restaurant in Los Feliz where we are so quiet, you kiss me because I had nothing to say.

14. San Francisco—that bar Specs, it has a piano. Let's stand around it until poet Jack Hirschman shows up looking like a chef who just clocked out and is ready to eat everything. Kiss when his lines reach you.

15. Take the train from Fullerton. Do it on the day everyone moons the train. Kiss at your favorite ass.

16. What was the name of that bar in the movie; Chinatown, the one in San Pedro, hidden at the end of Gaffey Street, where the former road just crumbles off into the tide pools, the smash and graffiti of the dazzling cliffs? My life goes there, way down there when your kiss is full and sharp like a mustard burger, comes out at me as desperate as a last dollar. Walkers. I think it was Walkers.

PLACES YOU SHOULD NEVER KISS

1. In a Men's Warehouse, not the suit store. A warehouse where they make lousy men.

2. Conservative foam party. Not right wing conservative, conservative as in the soap is rationed so no one gets too fucky.

3. On the Peter Pan ride at Disneyland. Don't kiss while fake flying. Notice how you move over the darkness. Pay attention to tiny London. Tiny London is paying attention to you!

4. At a gun range after happy hour. Everyone you love is one bad joke away from leaving you for good.

5. In a city that doesn't get its own jokes.

6. Um. Never kiss someone who is searching for a word and tells you they are blanking. They will think you are putting words in their mouth. It's much worse.

7. In front of someone in Malibu with a sense of humor.

8. Inside of a literal white Russian. It must break you.

9. At a vegan BBQ while everyone compares the glisten of their fake meat sweats around the L.E.D. campfire, embracing the future, embracing a lack of joy until that becomes joy. Do not kiss them until they admit they are meat.

10. In a gay western seafood bar called Fish and Chaps.

11. You should never kiss someone who is trying to enjoy a churro. A churro is just a donut with a boner.

12. During a conversation at a party full of comedy improvers, which you thought were going to be improoovers, which was to be a positive step in the emotional reconstruction of Derrick Brown, but every conversation is powered by the improv rule "don't deny." So yes, I WILL have another drink with dumb ass fruit in it; and everyone will yes, wear their church pants into the above ground pool; and yes, you will drive us all home, or a place that has been waiting for you to name it home; and yes, you will nap lucid in a new un-cynical life of wet pants, bonus drinks, and learning to say yes. Put a towel on the seat. Get in. Take me home. I'm outta words. I'm blanking. Kiss me long war. Kiss me the opposite of cross fit. Kiss me Tennessee porch song. Kiss me assy. Kiss me dead as drugs. Kiss me lost. Kiss me gold in the sunrise. Kiss me all the way home.

MULE BREAKER

come to the blue
and find me.

come to the moss night.

come to the woods
loaded with the OCD
cicadas and their clickers.

cumberland river, naked.

red teeth calling.

you broken mule.

I still love you.

who is your armory?

what songs of ours can you still hear?

the radio tried to sell too much
to keep us listening.

I hear you
in every spinning fan blade.

in the hole peeking from the glued corner
of a dead man's mouth.

he sings
of the thing he wishes
he could see again
if he could fall asleep
in peace.

ODE TO MY VOYAGE ACCOMPLICE

For all the support you give, I will call you girdle.
You, my singing ally, my voyage accomplice.
streetlight dance partner, my constant casual Friday.
Bad head, Pez dispensing laughing spree.
I couldn't get your love off with a laser.

Let me coo in your bazazz.
Nothing is suddenly everything when I'm with you.
When you make me laugh, every good pair of underwear dies.
You are worth every minute shivering in the drunk tank.
They can't sell this feeling. They can't buy what we have.
In a world of lies and the hard sell, you are easy listening,
breeze through a bank orchestra, beautiful relic, jean piss bliss.

Stay with me like a jingle.
I may not have your looks, but I definitely have your back.

Citrus Woman! All your light is lime-light!
Thank you for all the cell phone radiation you endured
in our late night chats.

You're cool is so cool, oh shit, where'd all the global warming go?
You market tested better than free chocolate
and commercially appealing babies!
You grew tired of my poetry, so I told you-
Your eyes, so fuckable.
Tell the moon to stop sending you fan mail.
It makes her jealousy bright.

WHAT HAPPENED IN CHARLES
DE GAULLE AIRPORT

I lost her.

I took the voucher. To stay.
I just had to tell the gate.
I went through the clear security doors.
I told them, excitedly, that I would be staying.

They said, there must be some mistake, you must board now.
If you skip out on this ticket, you will have to pay another 2000 dollars.

I walked back to the clear wall.
You were sitting like a friend trying to stay awake
in a hospital.
You saw me, stood up, and smiled so big.
You couldn't hear me.
They wouldn't let you close.
I put my thumb down.

You cried fast, like a storm over Houston.
You mouthed, "why?"

I shook my head and turned towards the plane.
I wanted to say so much in the language you grew up on.
I can't believe they wouldn't honor the voucher to stay,
what a cruel mistake,
felt my heart strip the clutch.

I flew home and cried out every tiny bottle in my body
all the way back to the states.
I hate crying.
I knew why there was so much.

I knew it would take years
for me to make enough money
to come and see you again.

And I knew we couldn't last that long
without being touched.

KING LUDWIG TO RICHARD WAGNER

My hunger has turned on me.
My hunger is Kudzu.
My hunger swallows my heart meat first.

They will kill me when they find me,
Richard. I could not hold it in.
They will say I drowned.
This is true.

I drowned in your sonata.
Your mad love took me.

Desire cuts as the Rheine.
Hold my blood from the still water.
Hold your fingers to the ivory as I shake.

I will not sing out the useless breath
of how I needed you,
how I needed your sound.
I will go silent, weighed down
by the medals and crown.

Am I not man before I am King?
I daydreamed, and I lost.

They killed me for you,
and I let them.

You will grow old,
and you will see me in the Bavarian blue of every lake.
Your heart will fail you. It failed me too.

I hear Parsifal.
I hear Das Rheingold.
I hear Fantasia in F-sharp.

The water is waist deep.
There will be no inquiry.
Richard, I still hear.

I hear them coming for the me
that is already gone.

Every palace—a monument
to the wasted energy of men,
fools hoping the work of slaves
would instill a sense of honor for others,
reverence and beauty for what we can accomplish
when pushed.

All I wanted
was a voice by the fire.

HEY KID

Hey kid. Look. See the attractive couple stumbling from the airplane lavatory back to their seats? The man clutching his gut, pretending he was sick? The woman talking through her messed up blonde, bangs all huffing across her big smeared lips? Doesn't she look like a cross between Carly Simon and the Muppet who looked like Carly Simon?

Hey kid says, "Who's Carl Simon?" Salted airplane peanuts fall from the small hands between myself and his aisle seat.

Oh, Carly Simon was a '70s woman singer who was known for singing a song about vanity and how the subject of the song was about a vain dude, and the line in the song is *I bet you think this song is about you.* But she wouldn't say who she was singing about, so everyone thinks it's a song about them. It kind of makes you feel good knowing someone wrote a song for you even if it's not nice. At least you got a song?

The hey kid, splitting peanuts with his little teeth non-plussed. I am tempted to tell him that the couple wasn't sick and that they were mid-air boning and to go see which bathroom smells like a wet bag of pennies and shmutz so I don't have to use it.

I want to tell him what they were doing to see if I can explain why. I don't do it. I am envy. I am not sure why people get a kick out of love in weird places. I want to begin writing the history of award winning, slutty summers. I want it to sound American and pissed. I'd have to make it up. Eloquent and well dressed, then repulsed and outside. Bill Hicks and Tom Wolfe together at last—7 minutes in heaven. Only one comes out.

Now I wonder about Moses 'cause I am old next to this pre-teen hey kid passenger, and he is reading a cool pocket Bible, splitting more peanuts, and I say:

Hey kid. If Moses and all the Jews really survived in the desert; and let's say maybe two magic trains totaling two miles in length arrived everyday to feed them; and let's say to eat the cooked food, two more trains with four thousand tons of firewood showed up since the desert has no flammable materials; and let's say 11 million gallons of water a day showed up for cooking anddrinking, which would take a train that was 1800 miles long; and let's say they loved this life and did this for almost fifteen thousand days, say that sounds super crazy or just crazy crazy?

He says, "I don't know. It was a miracle."

Do you like miracles, like believe in them now?

Hey kid teen says, "Yep. It's just more fun that way."

Exit science. Exit cynic. Exit mystery gloss. Exit upper class sneaky genitalia. I look out the window. Flight lends me an infinite concern for far away little things—swimming pools are tiny, sparkling rectangular crystals, are the things inside of salt.

I want to know even a small miracle and become brighter than space gold.

Hey kid. We, I mean scientists, just found out that gold comes from a collapsed star called a neutron star and came here on meteors. All the gold we have on this planet was born from the smash of dense stars billions of years ago. If you wear gold, you wear a piece of the most violent thing in our universe, a thing that was made in freaking outer space. Is that a miracle?

"Sure."

Hey kid doesn't say sure like a bored Sunday dad. He says it like he just saw the Grand Canyon one morning but works there and still isn't sick of it.

My travel size bottle of water. The contents lifted from the sea. Into the clouds. Into a machine to make it better. There were creatures moving in a drop of that water. Seventeen thousand drops in a gallon. Is that a miracle? Do those creatures need names? A man is directly in the middle between an atom and the entire galaxy. In the way? Exit pride.

Hey kid. When I look out this window and I think of our country, I think of the Army and I realize that the poor are protecting us; and I think a new law should be formed, that if war is voted for, a lottery must be held and 51% of all senators or their children or their wives will be asked to serve in combat arms; and we can welcome an age where there is a war where no one dies and everyone speaks as well as they can in a kind of love that ain't vain or cynical. A clear thing. A clear love. Wouldn't that be better? Wouldn't it be a miracle if we could talk and not slice each others throats?

Hey kid says, "I don't know. I know I like riding my bike, and I really like pizza. I don't love it. You shouldn't always say love. I love my sister. She hates pizza. You can say you hate anything. You shouldn't say you love everything."

Exit over-read bloodlust. The night comes on over the landscape like glitter catching light in a widow's bonnet. We are near DC.

Hey kid. I didn't know Arlington Cemetery used to be Robert E. Lee's rose garden. Then the Union took it over and made it a grave-site. How neat to take an enemy's place of serenity and bury all your friends there.

"Is that it down there?"

Yes. I think that's it.

"Sad. My cousin Anthony died. He was a musician. I am sad because he can't make music anymore, and we all loved his music."

Loved?

"Yeah. We loved his music."

We are flying over monuments becoming lit.

Hey kid. John Wilkes Booth caught his spur in the American flag and broke his leg after temporarily murdering a mountain. Exit the absence of poetry. Exit non-magic. Exit anti-miracle stuff. I am not sure why, but the more I look out this window, the more I feel like telling the stewardess I love her and the guy behind me and the woman reading *US Weekly*.
Ma'am, I love you. I said it too softly. Stewardess says, *Please bring your seat back up.*
Sir, I hate to interrupt, but I wanted to say I love you. Damn. I mumbled it. Man ignores me, adjusts his headphones, and makes DMV face.

Music up too loud.
Ma'am. Ma'am, I love you. Older Woman reading mag says, *I love you too. That's a funny thing.*
Where are you from?

Nowhere. I just wanted to say it. I felt compelled. I'd rather not talk 'cause now I feel weird.

You're fine, she says. *You're fine.*

Hey kid says, "Why did you tell those people you loved them?" I said 'cause there was no way in hell I would ever do something like that. If I did, it would be a small miracle. Kid, things are worse off everywhere else except for Switzerland, and they are bored and want graffiti and m-80s. I'm ready to try this miracle shit. I started thinking about stuff, looking down, and thinking about national stuff, and now I feel as alive as all sea lanes. It means nothing to that guy. Thanks for the uplift.

Kid says, "Thanks for telling me about Carly Simon. Should I look her up? Is she good?"

I like her music. I like that one song I guess.

I look out the window and remember a teacher saying:
Never write about explicit beauty, and never use the word love outright.
Find a synonym.
And never ever ruin a compliment by tacking on the word *finally*.

Looking out the oval, descending like something, I see the light of the countryside. I love you. Easy. You're beautiful.
Finally.

LAVA

Every coffee table, a fort
to some child
and you are amazed that
you too used to be a puddle of Thousand Island dressing
inside a ripe vagina
and then you were the size of a case of beer
and when you toddle-hugged someone you loved
so hard,
you could only reach
the tree stump of their leg
to slobber on
and they didn't shush you away.

Noise gusher.

What was wrong with young you?
How come your tongue so badly
wanted to be in every light socket?

How come your forehead
greeted every piece of cement
like an old friend?

How come your legs
weren't the synchronized model
you always wanted?

Who could love the mess?
Who could love a rig of rolling defeats?

You wanted
someone to find you like an unmapped island
to *safe* you
like a full gun at night in the sticks,
to want you
like chased meat,

to alter your dark, to change your doctrine
like a church of Christ that holds its first dance.

To lift you
like a voice that sings when you laugh like a mansion.

You were as misunderstood as Arkansas
and tried to summon Hawaii inside
'cause everything you loved
was stunning and distant.

Yeah, yeah, yeah, your dad stuff.

Some fathers pour their money and love into cars
because they were never taught how to slow the flood
so they just kept their hands moving,
building something
so they wouldn't give in to
tearing everything apart.

Some mothers look to the heavens
and sing out to the lord all day
waiting for a song to come back,
constantly looking up
so they don't have to remember
the dirt waiting for them and the ones they love.

I sing for the one who came to me.
I love you out there;

I love you out there; I love you beyond your bloodline,
the embrace of your shins,
the pillow between your legs
the spine against my chest curving like a modern tent post
as beauty becomes a covered feeling.

Come
like free weed when the cramps keep coming.
Stay
like flowers in the salt and daylight float of Oahu.

In Hawaii
the horrors of the volcanoes barfing up themselves
unto themselves
and unloading their mess

into beaches of black gold reminds me of you—
a horror cooling.

There is a drawing
in black and white
of an empty field of tree stumps,
clean cuts
that someone had chainsawed down,
and when I think of it, I cry.
I cry, not because it was drawn so well
or that beauty had slow blown its way in
like a scotch headache.

I weep because
it isn't the beauty others see first that lasts
but the beauty that someone, at sometime
catches if they wait.

The first time I looked at it,
I saw vast emptiness, loss of life.
When I came back to it,
I noticed in the corner
a silhouette of one person
staring over the empty hillside
with a noose in their hand.

I couldn't help but think of you.

You have done the heaviest of things.
You have changed my plans.

OUR POISON HORSE

The horse in our field.
The black one.
Our poison horse.

Why would anyone try to poison her?
They think boys wanted the flies on her dead.
That or the boys wanted to see the skin peel.

The pesticide scar,
healing now as the jagged underline
slowly closes daily
on the mare's body,
The underlining of everything awful
about us.

      I ask you if there is anything worth saving?

You land me
a kiss so hot
the ferns die.

A grip so tight,
the blisters
keep you from volunteering to carry
anymore coffins.

Broken fast
like an under chucked
snowball.

Lungs rising
like Dresden
steeples.

A kiss so hot
the butcher's meat
is ready.

You are
this coward's
drink,
a last drink
before
the bell rings
and the crowd wants blood
and the rafters spin.

Your face is leaking.
    You're the one permanent wedding.
I'm a teenage dog in the back of a truck.
I gotta jump. When will it slow down enough?

You tell me you love me,
and it unfolds my will
to live.

ACKNOWLEDGEMENTS

Poems have appeared in and special thank you to:

The Rattling Wall, Pank, Lunch Ticket, Going Down Swinging, The Nervous Breakdown, The Incredible Sestina Anthology, DM du jour, lit genius, Australian Broadcast Company, Paper Darts, Scene Missing, Empower Magazine, Wild Spice Mag, LA review of Books, Austin Chronicle, Brightest Young Things, Fields Magazine, Good Guy Publishing, Common Line Journal, Live Wire Radio, Entertainment For people, Austin American Statesman and Busted Mouth.

I have an awful memory, but as I write this, these images pop up. I am grateful to these people for lifting me up:

Amber Tamblyn. You literally saved my life. Maybe you figuratively did too. Thank you for running all the stop lights to keep me here.

Jessica Blakeley. You showed me how to love, when to love and when to get 'Philly.'

Irene and Dave Holmes. Thank you for sweating all over the Ranch Dressing.

Mr Marks, my Pacifica High School Drama teacher. You and Patty made me feel confident for the first time in my life.

Buzzy and Don Rogers for introducing me to magic and the joy of bad jokes.

Rob Zabrecky. I never thought I'd get into the Magic Castle or your heart, but here we are!

Jeffrey McDaniel. You told me I could do this. Then you showed me. You are the best poet in the world. I can't wait for the world to find out.

Cold War Kids. What a gracious thing of courage, inviting me to open up for your rock band on those tours. It could have blown so hard. I guess some nights it did. But it taught me so much about not being afraid of new shit and I am changed for it.

Amber Tamblyn and Matt Wignall duo. Remember when you and Matt Wignall flew all the way to Nashville and I was depressed and you both road tripped me home and helped me pack to move back to the west and you were on a new birth control pill and Matt was sick as hell and you rolled around on the asphalt in lower-lady-area pain and Matt was all pale and puking? I wished I knew what to do then to make you both feel better. Thank you for making me feel better.

The lady at the Clines Corners gas station in New Mexico on interstate 40, when I had been motorcycling in freezing rain for hours. I came in and you saw me, came to me, told me to remove my gloves. I thought it was cause I was getting merchandise wet. You warmed my hands in yours and it was a sweetness I'll never forget.

Bill Baumgart and Tim Ellis. You let me leave for tour to build my career and it changed my life for the better. Thank you for letting me sneak weird jokes into your Christian kids' TV show.

Mindy Nettifee. I miss you every day. We were poetry kids at Jamz coffee shop. What the hell happened?

David Cross. You gave me one of the biggest gigs of my life at All Tomorrow's Parties. You changed my life by introducing me to the nice people. You are kind and giving and I like that it's a secret. Thank you for enduring my face and for reading half of some of my poems. Sorry about leaving a peach pit in your shower. I thought fresh fruit and a hot shower would be a great combination. It is! But it makes you forgetful.

Jaimes Palacio. You do so much to bring poets together. I see it and am thankful. I felt honored to have a song on your Christmas CD.

Cristin O'keefe Aptowicz. You are who I turn to. Thank you for never turning away. You are a rock. A whole quarry. Let me be there when you have your first cocktail.

Ben Pearson. You make me laugh when I need it the most. You make me wanna dance like an idiot.

Bucky Sinister. My advice machine. Thank you for coming to the hospital. It meant so much.

Beau Sia. I love your tenderness. I love rap battling you with positivity.

Ross Szabo. Thank you for pushing yourself in marathons and in life. You are an inspiration for getting shit done.

Steve and Jen Lewis. You are forever Catalina Island now. Thanks for being more than a great party to me.

Anis Mojgani. 10-5 goodbuddy. You show me how to see the other side. In debates, in the fantastical. All the love you pour into your work, we feel it.

Curtis Luciani. If our shrinkwrap videos ever reach 500 hits, you owe me some chicken. Thank you for being a real barrel of sex.

Eric Guerreri. Your friendship is medicine. I love your spirit. Sorry about writing about your sperm.

Rachel Morrison. Keep the shoulder Shimmies coming or else.

Amy Poehler. I didn't know you could dance so hard.

Caitlin Moe. I see your skill and it makes me want to be better at art.

Adrian Wyatt. You still show me how to dream my ass off.

Geoff Lemon. You made me fall in love with your country. You gave me so much of your time, I apologize to your girlfriend. Thank you for being a pal. Hey look, a Joey! Dinner!

Simon Kindt. You left your family to show me the gold coast and as I swung on that vine in the rainforest, I feltso lucky. That clean bed meant so much to me.

Scotty Sneddon. Keep going man! You are changing people!

Blaine Fontana and Eugenie. You painted me flying on a fish and I see it everyday and love your example of teamwork and being mellow. I felt so proud seeing the art you made from the Butterfly Knife book.

Timmy Straw. That moment at the saloon in Likely, California was one of the most beautiful moments of my life, when your piano playing put the cowboy bartender in tears.

Emily Wells. Seeing you bunny hop is all the joy I need.

Dion Bellmare. Seeing you in your monster truck gear is a cherished feeling.

Travis Tohill. Stop moving away from me all the time! I'm trying to love you!

Joel Chmara. My tour partner, maker of Bears fans, maker of Chicago Chicago laughter, bad idea memory master. I love seeing you in a costume. Get to it.

To Meghann Plunkett. Thank you for being made from future cotton candy and baby tears.

To Angry Sam. After they almost stabbed me in Hackney, you chilled my out by teaching me Cricket. Thank you.

Diana Shattuck. I didn't pack out the Opera House and you still told me it was a success. Thank you for being a champion for poetry and easy kindness.

Bohdan Piasecki. My far away friend. Thank you for lifting poetry up onto your shoulders. You do so much and we owe you beer forever.

Josh Grieve. Thank you for letting me my a chonus in your dangus and for makingwhite wine rhyme with shrimp. I love your talent.

Baz. I can still see you up in the balcony, throwing tennis balls at poets and it makes me smile to this day.

My family. We are weird. Now I accept it and I like it.

Rayne Sieling. Thank you for your beautiful, unfurling adventure style heart.

Ashley Siebels. Your perfect brain and creative power strip saved write bloody. I owe you a sandwich. Thank you for sharing your goods.

Shea Newkirk. Someday I will pay you what you deserve. I am so grateful for the tech skills you share with a bunch of broke ass poets.

Lea Deschenes. You helped build this tiny company, write bloody. Few may know the brilliant and tedious work of layout that you pulled off and all the headaches that come with that. We were lucky to have you. I hope that doesn't sound like you are dead. Cause you are not. Nor will you ever be.

Keaton Maddox. You are the master mind of free beer Friday. Thank you for bringing your gay ass brain to the party.

Andrea Gibson. Thank you for getting funny and for eating. I like what you've done with your hair.

Grimey and Drew. You took a chance and booked a poet at the basement and mercy lounge. You also gave birth to the spring hill spider party. The world is still pissed.

The Valentine family. You all carried me when I busted my ankle. I felt like a sissy. Thank you for making sissy feel so good.

James Valentine. Thank you for letting me meet Katy Perry in your pool when I was at my fattest.

Amanda Valentine. Thank you for the best jacket of my life. Hell yes it had tails!

Write Bloody authors. Thank you for giving a shit and being an author who meets the fans. So many writers are boring and lifeless onstage, then they seem like they loathe meeting people or signing books. Seeing Sarah Kay or Karen Finneyfrock greet people post show with huge smiles makes me feel like we won.

Richard Swift. Hearing you play the organ while the dryer was going and eating all the tequila was a time that I felt so lucky to be working with someone so gifted. Thank you for being a bit off.

Beau Jennings. I love the music that still waits inside you. Thank you for your endless couch.

Hamish Ramsay. You are a beautiful dude. And yes, that is flirting.

Olivia Wingate. I feel your belief in me and it makes me proud. I also love your tiny glasses.

Taylor Mali. You are still ziplining across my friggin heart and I am still sore! Thank you for giving me all your money. Thank you for making poetry fun and thoughtful for millions.

Brendan Constantine. The poet laureate of future jungles. I love your head.

Jeremy Radin. Aren't you the best new person? Whenever people meet you, there is a reason that you are their new favorite person. Is it the pee stains on your skivvies? Nope. It's something else. I'm sure of it.

Kelly Brown. Hang in there, my friend. Amarillo needs you. All hail your bitchin spirit!

Josh Boyd. Let me hear that great giggle that you got on repeat and I'll be just fine.

Jay Buchanan. You inspire me. Not just to poop, but to keep going on the road.

Daniel Lisi. I am ready to intern for you, my friend. Your loyalty changed our company. We are friends for life and I know that's a substantial burden, but it's just the way it is. I have seen how you work and I am awed by how you can do anything. Why not start with the dishes?

Jene Guiterrez. You give so much. And now I deed you the moon!

Paul Frank Sunich. You loaned me your classic car when I was all outta moneyand wheels. it meant so much.

The Guy in Nebraska. To the fella that handed me a 100 dollar bill when my van broke down on tour, I still do that to this day if i meet a touring band down on their luck. Thank you.

Heather Knox. Thank you for your advice when I needed it the most. Your comments turned this manuscript down a better road and I felt so stuck.

June Melby. Thank you for the bonking sound.

Ellen Maybe. I think of your smile all the time. Do you floss with the 1960's?

The Howze Brothers. Are you too tall to have me kiss you anymore? Look at you!

Kurt Braunohler. You make me want to try big things. Not like, tall dudes, but your skywriting idea still lingers in my head about the joy of a fresh approach.

Elna Baker. You gave me a compliment one time about something, maybe my clothes or something and I'll never forget it.

Buddy Wakefield. Your laugh is big as fuck. I need it. Oh and you are healed. All done!

Interns. Thank you for donating a chunk of your life for poetry.

The city of long beach.

The house party 2 band. You know what you did.

Azure Parsons. Thank you for your power.

GregDulli. Youmayhaveadickforabrain,butyoualsohaveabig,beautiful country dick for a heart. Wait. I am saying thank you for constant inspiration and your good poetics locked inside of rock action.

The person I forgot. I was trying. I was really trying. I got a weird, drifty mind.

For the dancers in Groningen, the beautiful little town in a Dutch sea of mayonnaise where tall people hold hands while riding bikes, where dance parties at French Martin's house turn into graffiti festivals, where Stephen Shropshire poured out his love and Bruce poured out his patience on the floor for the beautiful Aimee to electric slide in, where a bunch of mad dancers came and held each other up on their shoulders when their legs gave out, where the music of Emily Wells and Timmy Straw flowed like cold La Chouffe, we will miss each other, all us wolves, farmers, and witches. Recalling that all great and lasting love is rarely face to face. May you remember the audiences you transform. May you challenge the heavens, the rules and forever be transformed, kinda like Roy.

Eugene Mirman. This book is for you because you pulled me out of the mud when I was feeling the walls closing in. To you it might have been another tour, hitting the road and touring for some fun but I was feeling in the dumps and needed a spark. I had no idea how the comedy world would take poetry, or if they would endure it because they loved you. It felt like they loved it and it revitalized my belief that poetry is for the working class and isn't just for academics thrilled at whacking each other off. Does that sound like they are killing each other? Thank you for taking a chance on this dude and for literally changing my path. I can never repay you, so don't ask.

photo by Jessica Blakeley

ABOUT THE AUTHOR

DERRICK c. BROWN is the winner of the 2013 Texas Book of The Year award for Poetry. He is a former paratrooper for the 82nd airborne and is the president of one of what Forbes and Filter Magazine call "...one of the best independent presses in the country", Write Bloody Publishing. He is the author of four books of poetry. The New York Times calls his work, "...a rekindling of faith in the weird, hilarious, shocking, beautiful power of words." He lives outside of Austin, TX in a sweet, tiny country town called Elgin, TX. Brownpoetry.com

WRITE BLOODY BOOKS

After the Witch Hunt — Megan Falley

Aim for the Head, Zombie Anthology — Rob Sturma, Editor

Amulet — Jason Bayani

Any Psalm You Want — Khary Jackson

Birthday Girl with Possum — Brendan Constantine

The Bones Below — Sierra DeMulder

Born in the Year of the Butterfly Knife — Derrick C. Brown

Bouquet of Red Flags —Taylor Mali

Bring Down the Chandeliers — Tara Hardy

Ceremony for the Choking Ghost — Karen Finneyfrock

Clear Out the Static in Your Attic — Rebecca Bridge & Isla McKetta

Courage: Daring Poems for Gutsy Girls — Karen Finneyfrock, Mindy Nettifee
& Rachel McKibbens, Editors

Dear Future Boyfriend — Cristin O'Keefe Aptowicz

Dive: The Life and Fight of Reba Tutt — Hannah Safren

Drunks and Other Poems of Recovery — Jack McCarthy

The Elephant Engine High Dive Revival anthology

Everyone I Love Is A Stranger To Someone — Anneleyse Gelman

Everything Is Everything — Cristin O'Keefe Aptowicz

The Feather Room — Anis Mojgani

Floating, Brilliant, Gone — Franny Choi

Gentleman Practice — Buddy Wakefield

Glitter in the Blood: A Guide to Braver Writing — Mindy Nettifee

Good Grief — Stevie Edwards

The Good Things About America — Derrick Brown and Kevin Staniec, Editors

The Heart of a Comet — Pages D. Matam

Hot Teen Slut — Cristin O'Keefe Aptowicz

I Love Science! — Shanny Jean Maney

I Love You is Back — Derrick C. Brown

CPSIA information can be obtained
at www.ICGtesting.com
Printed in the USA
FSOW02n0138160415
6382FS